A Grumpy Guide to Building Your Own Off-Grid Home

Will Penney

First published 2018

Copyright ©2018 Will Penney

All rights reserved. No part of this publication may be reproduced, stored in a retrieval system or transmitted in any form or by any means electronic, mechanical, photocopying, recording or otherwise, without the prior permission of the author, except in the case of brief quotations embodied in critical articles and reviews.

Introduction

If you have ever picked up a self-help book, or a building renovation manual, or even a home maintenance/D.I.Y handbook, you will know that it all looks terribly straightforward and presented to appear within the scope of even the most ham-fisted, impractical types, "why don't we all cut out the trades people, it's so simple," we are encouraged. When you reach the realms of environmental projects or eco-homes, the enthusiasm verges on gushing.

But if you have ever taken, or intend to take, the bold step beyond dreaming, planning and visualising, onto the rollercoaster of actually doing it, then you may find that things aren't as straightforward as they seem.

As you variously go through stages of idealism, hope, despair, tantrums, fulfilment, fatigue and just plain grumpyness, you may appreciate that this is quite normal for mere mortals like us who have never really tried anything like this before.

To give the less rosy side of the story, here is the grumpy guide to building an off grid, eco-home, or in other words, the full, real-life story of a couple trying to provide a sustainable place to live without harming the World, this is our story.

Chapter 1 – Diggers and Dreamers

So Janet and I were, are, volunteer Greenpeace activists living in the UK. We've spent years banging on about how we need to change our attitudes to the environment and need to tread a lighter path if we are to pass onto our children a World worth living in.

Janet has a degree in the subject and even taught in schools. Both of us have been arrested for taking peaceful direct action, we feel so strongly about it.

Sometime around 2010, possibly after the COP15 climate summit in Copenhagen where we marched 100,000 strong to watch our 'leaders' fail us, we realised that simply telling people wasn't enough, society wasn't making the changes required within the necessary time frame and the World was going down. People didn't even seem to mind that this meant their darling offspring would undoubtedly struggle to survive the century, just so long as they could watch X-Factor then what did the future matter?

I think it's fair to say that we have despaired of the human race and decided that we do not wish to be part of the destruction that humans are exacting upon the natural world as it systematically eradicates habitats and species.

We both visualised a rural self- sufficient smallholding as the future we wished to realise for ourselves.

Admittedly, with a population of 60ish million, not everyone in the UK could follow our example but there is an element of self preservation within our project. Smallholdings can provide local food for their rural communities, with better livestock welfare and personal care and attention to every aspect of their holding. Whilst people in cities have to rely on imports that could not be guaranteed.

But enough of the doom and gloom, let's get on with the grumpy building stories.

No, first we have the fun bit of planning the whole set up from scratch and dreaming of the good life when it all comes together.

Where?

Janet is from the north of England, I'm from the south and we both had family considerations so somewhere in the middle would work well.

Land to the west was cheaper than land to the east, in fact the only place we could afford to buy a few acres was Wales.

Even with this in consideration a house with land was beyond our pocket.

We went on a smallholding course run by Simon Fairlie, we were expecting to learn all about the practicalities of running a small farm but ended up spending almost the entire weekend talking about getting planning permission to build.

Simon belongs to an organisation called Chapter 7 and is a bit of a planning maverick, a nightmare for local authorities and a hero for low impact subsistence farmers.

He argued that policies for genuine applicants wishing to start smallholdings in the countryside, were in place and should be pursued.

Wales had just heralded a new progressive policy called One Wales, One Planet, including a planning policy called One Planet Development no doubt prompted by Pembrokeshire's Low Impact Development Policy 52 and the successful application of the Lammas eco-community.

In short, if you can prove that your ecological impact falls within, or headed significantly towards, a footprint that could be provided by one planet, instead of approximately three which is the average for people in this country, then you could build in the open countryside;

so long as it's all totally reversible,

so long as it's only for yourselves,

so long as you have no significant environmental, landscape, transport or community impacts,

so long as it's zero carbon in construction and use,

so long as you can provide an income from your land to meet your minimum needs,

so long as you produce at least 30% of your own food,

so long as you manage to assimilate very nearly all your waste,

so long as you provide annual monitoring reports,

so long as you write a robust management plan which is renewed every 5 years,

so long as you can persuade your overworked local planning officer to take the time to learn about this strange new policy and having to deal with people who couldn't afford expert reports so were going around writing the things themselves and ultimately the monitoring of the monitoring reports!

If you manage to negotiate the 71 page practice guidance and come out the other side thinking you can do it, congratulations. You are about to embark on journey where people will laud you as a pioneer as you bang your head against a brick wall of bureaucracy based on financial values rather than ecological ones.

This is the road we set off down. As so often happens in Wales, the road turned into a track and the track ended at a farm gate with a Collie barking furiously at you whilst you wonder whether the whole idea was a good one in the first place.

We searched for the right piece of land for about 18 months.

Along the way we undertook numerous trips all over Wales, often making them into little camping holidays. One such trip was to look at a decent little patch of woodland with a small field beyond, trouble was it was close to Hay-on-Wye which is quite a posh area. It went to auction with a guide price of £55-£75,000. We could just about afford it but only if we sold our flat and no doubt would have to get a crippling bridging loan in the meantime, so we went along and arrived at the auction early. Only a handful of properties were being sold and we nervously chatted to the auctioneers.

People started to drift into the village hall where it was being held, old fellas in Tweed, rotund farmers in wellies, couples looking serious, a small tribe of hippies and business men pulling up in BMWs. A strange collection interested in this land which was to be the last of the 3 lots on offer.

And so the time came to bid. I don't remember the other two lots, they were gone and my throat went dry.

Bidding started at £55,000, quickly rose to 70,000, then stalled, now was my time, as I went to raise my hand, one the hippies sat at the front stuck theirs up for the first time. Oh, I wondered, have they got the same thing in mind as us?

They were quickly outbid and away went the race again, 75, 80, 85, okay we're out now, we couldn't go beyond £80k really.

It was the hippies bid at £90,000 when a plummy voice asserted itself from the back of the room,

"100,000" it shouted, grimly the hippies looked at each other (we were rooting for them by now), took a deep gulp and bid 105.

"120" came back the plummy voice. That was it, no one was arguing with that kind of buying power and plummy voice took it.

I later found out that the voice belonged to the land owner adjoining the woodland. He had horses.

It seemed like the right bit of land was an elusive holy grail, perhaps it would never show up?

Going back over places which we had previously discounted, there was 14 acres of rough pasture within the Brechfa forest, it wasn't quite what we wanted, it was quite steep and access was down a mile long bridleway. There wasn't really much woodland on it to fuel the stove we were planning but maybe enough. It was right in the forest though and the views were stunning. We decided to go for it.

By coincidence a tiny terraced house in a nearby village came up for sale at a ridiculously cheap price (for a quick sale).

By emptying bank accounts and raiding savings, we were able to get both thereby setting up the springboard to our new life.

A few weeks later, I was still, out of habit, browsing the estate agents websites when another piece of land caught my eye.

It was on the edge of a village, 8 acres of gentle pasture, 5 acres of woodland, it could be the land we were so long looking for, the holy grail. Even though we had just completed the other purchases, I had to go and see it.

It was ideal and even the neighbour I spoke to wouldn't mind us building a small home there.

Why is it that when you face a difficult decision, it's not until you've made it that it all becomes clear and clearly you've made the wrong choice?

How on earth were we going to be able to buy this land as well? We still part owned a small flat in Oxfordshire, which despite it being one of the last places in Oxfordshire that anyone wanted to live in, it being Oxfordshire meant it was still worth a lot of money, although selling it would be challenging.

I'm not really sure how we did manage it, but by some curious financial juggling, extra loans, raiding parents savings, selling everything we had and even doing the conveyancing myself, we ended up with an excellent bit of land, a crap bit of land, a small terraced house, a dubious flat and a huge debt.

The following year was spent moving into the house, looking for work, selling the flat and paying off loans. Digging land drains, writing a tortuous management plan and trying to sell the 14 acres we didn't want.

Chapter 2 – Planning

With no money to appoint an agent, I sat down to research all that was needed to submit our planning application. I sometimes, no, I often think that these things are purposely designed to be beyond the abilities of lay people, generating specialist and lucrative businesses.

We met with the Planning Officer for an informal chat, it was clear he wasn't keen on us doing a One Planet Development. He seemed to regard the monitoring that planners would need to undertake with cynicism.

Our business was based on the production of high quality wool. This is agriculture and we could have gone down the new rural enterprise route but we believed in OPD so we persevered.

In May we submitted our application for a 16m x 5m timber clad, single storey home of straw bale construction. After some initial issues, it was validated.

We waited.

We attended the village community council meeting where our application was discussed. There were some concerns about access but in the end no serious objections were made. Phew, at least the locals aren't going to railroad us out of the village!

Next we met with the planning officer, again, and he said that he had concerns about certain aspects of our application but didn't elaborate. He did however say he would get back to us with them.

So we waited.

Summer came …. and went.

We waited.

We emailed the planning officer. No reply.

We wrote a letter to the planning officer, explaining that we were gathering more information that may address his concerns if he would let us know what they were. He replied – by email – saying that he would get back to us early next week.

We waited.

Autumn brought a colourful change of leaves but no response from the planning officer.

We had complied with our side of the contract, we had filed an application and paid the Council £300 to make the decision but they had not fulfilled their side.

So as the last days of dry weather headed for the hills, we decided to withdraw from the process and go ahead and build.

As I write this, 18 months after having our application validated, we still have not heard from the Council.

It would be totally off-grid and packed with innovation, in other words, although we tried to meticulously plan everything we could, there was an awful lot that would be made up as we go along.

Here's how we got on.

Chapter 3 – Build, stage 1

First off we needed somewhere to live on the land. So we bought a caravan off Ebay, being assured it didn't leak even though it was 25 years old. It was about 30' long so it would give us a little room to live in whilst building.

We towed it to our little field, dug a hole at the top of the field, which soon filled with water and laid a pipe down to a large tank by the 'van. This was to be our washing water. Drinking water would be brought from the house in re-used spring water bottles.

We got three large, 2nd hand, 170w solar panels, a charge controller and two large deep cycle batteries (2nd hand from a data centre).

Around the middle of September, we moved in. The caravan leaked.

We had been discussing construction methods with a friend called Anthony (more of him later) and he recommended a round wood timber frame design with straw bale in-fill. This has the advantage of being able to get the frame up and roof on within a few days, then you can work in the dry underneath. The strength of the building is in the frame, and it would look gorgeous.

So I went to see Anthony's mate Tom in Bristol who would build the frame in his workshop and then send it over to us dismantled for us to put together. It all looked great but I knew there would be a cost involved.

The quote came back at £5,000, which was really good and I knew he had heavily discounted it because he was keen to do a house.

The trouble was the planning permission, the whole thing could be interrupted and there was the possibility of having to remove the house once built. This meant that the frame would be adding £5,000 of risk. The frame would still retain value, even if it all had to come down, but that would depend on dry storage, finding a buyer or re-using it ourselves for something else.

Throughout the build, this consideration came back time and again, when a decision came between an expensive bit of kit that was tried and tested or something that would do the job but might not last, we went with the cheaper option – because we never knew if a planning officer would suddenly appear and close the whole project down.

So we decided to go with a load bearing design, that's where the straw bales themselves take the weight of the roof and provide structural strength to the walls, a bit like giant bricks and we bought a book. 'Building with Straw Bales, a practical guide for the UK and Ireland' by Barbara Jones.

I don't really regret the decision, having regard for how we came to it, but with hindsight, the frame would probably have been the better choice.

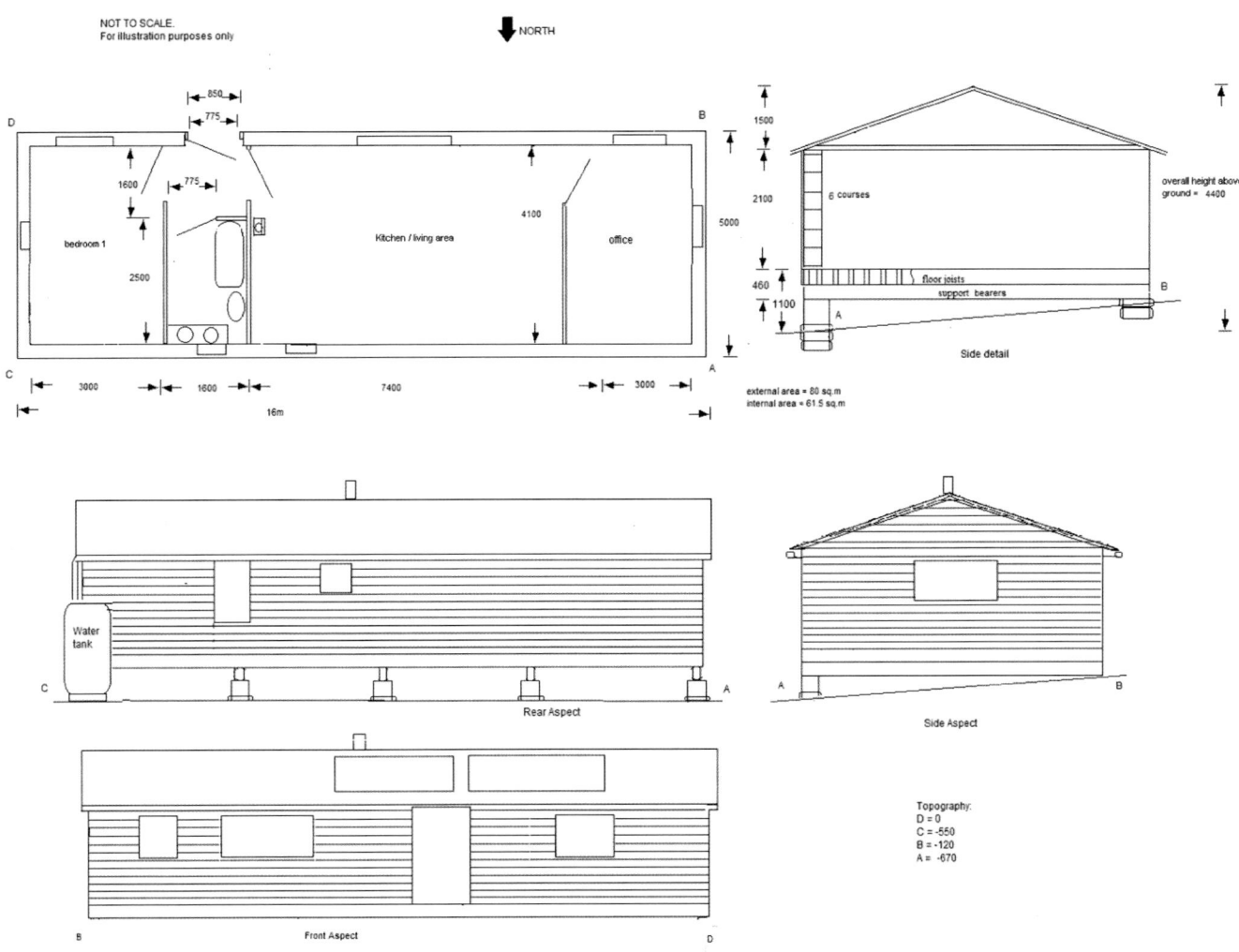

We started by digging 15 holes in the ground. About 2' deep. That night it rained, they filled with water. Our heavy clay soil has an amazing ability to retain moisture meaning that even the smallest crumb can dam a stream.

Into the holes we splashed car tyres and arranged 4 tonnes of stones to be delivered from a local builders merchants.

About 3 tonnes was to go into the reed beds for grey water treatment which we were building to a design from the Centre of Alternative Technology, the remaining filled the car tyres.

These pads rose just above the ground level, 3 lines of 5 holes, filled with car tyres, filled with stones. This is what the house would sit on, it's foundations if you like.

As the ground sloped away a bit, the downhill pads would need extra pilings to create a level platform. This was achieved by cutting 8 x 4" sleepers into blocks and building them up, Jenga style, on top of the rear pads to reach the levels of the uphill pads. Of course there were also pads in the middle which also had to line up, plus the ground also sloped slightly away to one end, so you can see, it wasn't exactly so straightforward. A number of hours were spent puzzling over lines and spirit levels but in the end the discrepancies were whittled down to 'as near as makes no difference'.

Then beams, the same 6 x 4 sleepers that had been cut for us by a nearby sawmill, were laid on to the pads so that one beam would sit on the front pad over to the middle one, and a second would sit from the middle pad to the rear one.

10 beams made up the structure that would support the building.

At this point, as I looked at it, I started to worry, as the beams were laid in their strongest orientation with the 8" side vertical, about the possibility of the whole thing rolling sideways. Sense told me that the weight of the building would surely hold it down, but I needed to be sure, this wasn't something I wanted even the slightest chance of happening once we were inside. Also there could be a strong possibility of needing to convince building inspectors at some point.

So we dug 5 pits alongside the beams, down about 30", right into the solid clay and stuck vertical posts (same sleepers again) in, rammed home and then fixed to the beams with threaded bars.

So far so good, the weather was turning increasingly unsettled but a dry spell was forecast so we cracked on with the platform.

Onto the beams we rolled out geo-textile, the stuff you might use to stop weeds growing up through your newly laid path, the idea of this was to insulate the wire mesh which was the next thing to be rolled out onto the beams, to try to prevent condensation. It looked simple enough, turned out to be a nightmare of course, the textile was 2m wide, the wire (1/2" galvanised chicken wire, to try to prevent vermin) was 1.5m wide. So the fabric went on first, up and over each beam, nailed in place, fine then how do we unroll the wire without treading on the fabric which towards the rear was about 3' off the ground. Where were the skyhooks and parachute harnesses when you need them? We ended up walking all over the fabric, tearing the nails through and making a bit of a mess of it, reasoning that it could be made good again after.

Next came the floor joists. According to Building Control span tables, we would need 195 x 47mm joists, with struts mid length and doubled up under weighty stuff like the side walls, bath, water tank and stove.

But here we had a dilemma, do we get the local sawmill to cut us the lengths or buy structural grade timber?

Our preference for locally sourced timber led us to the sawmill, but our concerns for potential Building Inspector appeasement finally took us to ordering a large quantity of (expensive) graded floor joists from a local building merchants.

Along the way, we did get a few of 8 x 2" (very nearly the same dimensions) from the sawmill and they were actually better quality. So much for doing the right thing!

Please appreciate that this build was running in a just-in-time fashion (more by default than design). This is a factory production technique of minimising costs and storage by getting everything to arrive just as you need it. Of course being an imperfect world, this seldom happens, meaning production lines stop for want of a small but vital bit that's got sent to the wrong factory or whatever and has to be expedited by courier. This ends up costing even more and ensuring that production managers spend all their time moving from one crises to the next.

Anyway, that's a different story and for me a different life.

Here we had no storage space, save a giant tarpaulin which was currently covering the straw bales like some white iceberg in the middle of the field.

The bales were one of the few things we bought in advance, way in advance as it turned out. The previous year we anticipated a cold winter and in Wales, where very little grain is grown, straw would be at a premium. For a load bearing straw bale wall, the best stuff is Barley straw as it compresses less that Wheat. Now the books tell you that you mustn't get straw which has any ears (seed carrying heads) still attached as the remaining grain will attract mice and rats. Yeah right. You try getting such material in a country that produces almost no straw, you have to go with what you can get.

As luck would have it, a farmer near our house (35 miles from the build site) also did a side line in straw and hay sales. During the previous summer, he had Barley straw, so we bought 270 small square bales at £3.20 each (yes they had plenty of ears attached). We found a local barn to store them over winter and transferred them to the field the next summer. As the sun shone down on our bales sweating under the tarp, some started to go mouldy. We ended up having to discard about 30 and buy replacements. Yet another little lesson learnt.

Back to just-in-time. Luckily for us most things for building a house are readily available so we could order and get deliveries fairly rapidly. Unfortunately for us, not all delivery lorries could make it up the farm track. So the generosity of neighbours allowing us to unload in their back yards, or at the bottom of the track, or even once at the train station, was appreciated. Where we could, we dashed off to get stuff on our slightly rickety trailer.

But with the tight timescale and the winter drawing in, this kind of scheduling was an extra burden.

In between the joists we laid 175mm of insulation. We decided upon a product called 'Earthwool', made from recycled glass, it was fire retardant and wouldn't be affected by moisture or damp.

13

Along with the joists were delivered the chipboard flooring. Not the most natural or eco solution but the most practical for the purpose and we did ensure it was FSC.

We still had flappy geo-textile under the joists which had to be nailed back in place by crawling underneath, in what was by now thick mud, in a space decreasing to less than a foot. Not fun.

Finally the chipboard was laid onto the joists. We found that chipboard and water don't go well together after a heavy downpour left us squeegeeing in an effort to keep it from swelling, followed by a rush to get to the next stage and get it covered.

So now the platform was ready, and it looked good. It felt like a stage, ready to take our next performance.

Chapter 4 – Build, stage 2

"Weather, weather altogether, what's it going to do? We don't know so let's ask weather man Emu", (Rod Hull and Emu, BBC TV).

Earlier in the year, we had stacked all the straw bales in the middle of the field, well actually more towards the bottom of the field than the middle wanting to minimise the distance we would have to carry them when construction started.

When we finally decided where we would build the house, we had moved it away from the trees more than originally expected and the bales were somewhat in the way. So one day I single handily moved the entire stack and nicknamed it bale mountain after stressing my arms and back.

Inside bale mountain also lay the remains of my sisters old kitchen units that we hoped to utilise. They were however, starting to deteriorate a little in the humid space under the tarpaulin and warp.

Now we were moving the lot again over onto the platform, creating a ridge down the middle so the tarp could cover everything and ensure the rain would run off.

It did rain but by raising one end of the tarp, I could work under it and prepare the wall plates that would sit on top of the bales.

These were made of 18mm orientated strand board (OSB sometimes called smart-ply), 8 x 4' sheets cut by the nice man at B&Q into strips 40mm wide. Down each long side went a length of 4 x 2" (from our friendly local sawmill). There was meant to be a second piece strip of OSB nailed on top to form a box but I figured the same could be achieved with less expense by nailing several short noggins of 4 x 2" between the previously mentioned lengths to brace them and in effect this worked.

There were only 2 of us working on this, Janet and myself, so I had to keep these wall plates to a length that we could both lift.

By significantly overlapping the 4 x 2's on the OSBs I figured the joins would tie in together. As it turned out, the bales being all slightly different heights, rather than being a rigid straight frame, the wall plates rose and fell like gentle waves over our sea of straw. If anyone questions why our roof turned out a bit wibbly-wobbly, this is why and given the restrictions we were facing, it couldn't really be avoided. Of course, if we had machines, hi-abs, cranes, people, unlimited time etc. it could have been better, but we didn't, so there!

Back to those pesky wall plates. They would be tied to the floor joists, sandwiching the straw bales, by 2" wide ratchet straps, so the next job was to cut holes in the flooring and put the straps in place ready while we could still easily access the joists.

In between the holes, under where the external walls would be, were placed 40mm strips of OSB. This is what the bales would sit on, a floor plate if you like, and would raise the straw a little off the surface layer to avoid damp from spillages, mopping, etc. This actually turned out to be very helpful later on.

Into the edges of the OSB I cut notches that would later take the 4 x 2" uprights holding the windows and door. All these had to be accurately cut and aligned. Not that it mattered much as in the end the bales were thrown up at such speed that the accuracy and alignment was all but lost. Why were they thrown up at such speed? Well what happened was…

The weather forecast was for a dry window of 4 days in the coming week. Ideally the straw bales need to be kept dry. When they get wet, they get mouldy and you don't really want to start living in a new house with mouldy weak walls.

As it wasn't at the time actually raining, we decided to put down the first 2 courses of straw bales. Eventually there would be 6 courses giving an internal height of 2.1m.

All good so far.

We covered it all back over with the giant tarpaulin. Janet went to do her weekend shift as a receptionist at a care home and I sat in the caravan watching as the heavens opened.

On the Saturday, the forecast now said there would be 3 dry days next week. It was still raining.

On the Sunday, the forecast said there would now only be 2 dry days next week. Bugger. It was still raining.

Monday arrived, Janet returned and the rain almost stopped.

The forecast now only gave us 1 dry day. I phoned everyone I knew who may be available to help at such short notice but no luck, we were on our own.

The next day dawned bright and clear, the sun shone and we worked like crazy to get the walls finished – hence the inevitable loss of niceties like plumb lines and levels and even a complete window!

We had planned a lovely full height quadruple glazed (2 x double glazed units) window into the kitchen area, but the distance between the window and the door was too small, only about 3 bales long, every time we built that section of wall, it fell over. Three times we tried, three times it wobbled and fell, once on us! So we gave up on it and built a longer stronger wall.

Now at this point I would like to point out that working with straw is not the joy some people seem to think.

Certainly walls can be built quickly and with only a little expertise. Along with a bale re-tying technique, you can achieve a lot with straw bales. For days after you will be pulling bits of it out of hair, crevices etc. For weeks you will be pulling it out of your clothes and months sweeping it up off the floor. It gets everywhere, it's dusty and goes mouldy if damp but the worst thing about it is the multitude of tiny abrasions it gives your hands – especially around the fingernails. The cut ends of straw can be really sharp. Wearing gloves can work for picking them up, throwing them around, but for squaring the ends, shaping or shortening them (the painful stuff), gloves don't give you the grip required.

I ended up disliking the straw. Not strongly, just a bit.

It was late afternoon by the time the last bales were lofted into place. Long hazel poles with sharpened ends had been hammered in down through the bales, (where we remembered to do so in the race against time) pinning them together. Corners interlocking and tied together with twisted hazel staples, a bit like thatching spars. I had made these staples up beforehand and most were too short, they needed to be at least 18" along the top with 6-9" down each side or spike. Even then they seemed to have limited value as the straw tends to be aligned across the bale giving little but the compressive force and the twine to hold the staple in. Also by the time you reach the higher courses, the unevenness of the bales tends to leave the staples at odd angles onto which the next course does not sit comfortably. Maybe with time these kind of fiddley details can be worked out but time is something we had run out of.

A breathable, but waterproof, membrane was then wrapped around the outside of the bales in 3 overlapping, 1.5m horizontal strips, kept in place with the plastic pins that came with the geo-textile used earlier.

After a good deal of internet research and comparing material properties against price we had decided on using Permavent for the membrane, (we needed it to be highly breathable but strong). They sent us Multivap 250. After more internet research and a phone call or two, we were reassured that it was essentially the same stuff.

Then, with a good deal of straining and struggling, we lifted the wall plates into place, capping the bale walls. Fixing the 4 x 2's together as Janet looped the ratchet straps over the top.

There were 20 straps along all the walls, each hooked under the outer floor joist, over the wall plate and back down to the inner floor joist, basically tying the whole structure together. Following the advice from the book we were informed that once we ratcheted it all down tight, the walls would transform into strong, solid structures. It did not however tell us where to put the ratchets, so not thinking too hard about it, we put them along the outside walls so that they would eventually be hidden behind the outer timber cladding.

The crowning moment came as the last of the evening light faded.

We ratcheted down all the straps, one by one, all of the walls started to lean outwards, pulled over by the force of the ratchets being on the outside.

Loosening them all, we pulled every other strap over so that the ratchet was on the inside.

We tightened the inner ones first then the outers. Most of the walls pulled back up vertical but one wall in particular remained stubbornly slanted. We would have to leave it for now and ordered more ratchet straps.

My advice for future reference, would be to position the ratchets on the top of the wall plate therefore exerting an even pull on both sides.

Now the challenge was to waterproof it before the rain came tomorrow.

We built several towers of spare bales with 4 x 2's running between them. A haphazard matrix of timber struts to try to give some pitch to the tarp which we hauled over the top. This tarp, by the way, was 16m x 10m and weighed something like 75kgs.

We eventually finished lashing it down and tuned in at midnight.

The next day was awful.

We woke in the middle of the night, well early hours of the morning really to the sound of rain on the caravan roof. It's a sound I came to truly hate and not only because the caravan leaked.

A sense of dread descended as dawn broke, we ate breakfast and braced ourselves for the coming day.

The rain was now harder than ever as we peered in to see the tarp leaking, everywhere.

The pitch of the timbers were not enough and the water was pooling and forcing it's way through tiny holes in the 190gm plastic sheeting. The floor was soaked, the bales were getting splashed, we didn't know what to do.

Grabbing all the buckets we could find, including the one we had been using for a toilet, we tried to catch as much as we could, working as a relay team emptying them outside.

We tried to push the sagging tarp up to clear the pools but the water was just too heavy.

There was a real danger that the weight of all the collected water would pull the walls inwards so we decided to puncture the tarp and let the water through, in some kind of controlled deluge, catching as much as we could in the buckets.

It wasn't average rain, it was that proper substantial stuff. The sort that requires fast windscreen wipers when driving.

We redoubled our efforts relaying full buckets for empty ones and felt like crying.

Somehow, in the middle of this, I managed to pick up the video camera and filmed a short sequence, just to remind us, as the mind quietly and quickly erases such traumatic memories, of just how bad it was.

Meanwhile, the roof trusses turned up. I clearly remember Janet, myself and the lorry driver all clad in plastic waterproofs hand-balling the timbers off as the rain pelted down.

We had decided upon pre-made trusses over a constructed roof for speed and convenience, plus the fact that I didn't know how to build a roof anyway. I ordered 10 trusses as the tin roof would be especially lightweight and I would tie them together with horizontal purlins.

Looking back at it now, we were building in what turned out to be the wettest winter on record (for England and Wales records go back to 1766) which was followed by one of the warmest ever summers! We could have saved ourselves a lot of heartache if we had known this before we started, which of course, we couldn't have done and now we were at a critical stage.

As we ate lunch in the caravan, the rain was easing off and the forecast improving. What should we do?

We had two options, carry on or write off the bales and wrap up the project until spring.

We were aware this decision would be a pivotal moment and we both felt like throwing in the towel for now, coming back when the weather improves.

But, I rationalised, what if we put in one last ditch, all out, single day of hard work? All we had to lose was our time, effort and perhaps our sanity.

It was a close call but in the end we decided that we would see if over the next 24 hours, we could get to a stage where the interior could dry out without too much damage. If not then we could then still wrap it all up. At over £800, the straw bales would be the greatest loss but if we couldn't dry it out then they would already be gone.

That afternoon the rain stopped but the forecast was uncertain.

We set about trying to remedy the leaning wall of straw.

Ratchet straps just weren't doing it so we poked a rope through the wall between the bales, tied it around a length of 4 x 2 on the outside, threaded the rope through the interior, out of a window and onto the bull bars of a Landrover. Then we winched it until the 4 x 2 threatened to pull through the wall. The wall slowly came upright. We released the tension. The wall leaned back out.

We winched again. The wall came upright. We paused and scratched our heads. Then we scratched our arses. We needed a way of holding it in place. So it was decided upon a quick trip to the nearest hardware shop to get a couple more ratchet straps whilst the Landrover held the straining wall upright.

With the extra straps firmly pulling on the inside and two lengths of 4m long 4 x 2's nailed right across the top tying the opposite wall plates to each other, we released the tension and the wall stayed upright, mostly, enough.

Then off came the tarpaulin and on went the roof trusses. Already the daylight was slipping away so we donned head-torches and carried on, not knowing what weather the following day would bring. With the trusses on there would be enough pitch and rigidity to shed any rain.

The trusses were fixed using metal brackets onto the wall plates. We marked out the gaps but in the darkness, working off ladders, it was almost impossible to tell how vertical everything was. We soldiered on with grim determination.

I remember it being a clear night and watching the Moon rise, gauging the passage of time by how far across the sky it had moved. By the time we had finished erecting the trusses and fixing the cross bracing, the Moon was sinking below the trees. I asked Janet what time it was and was slightly shocked to hear "half three".

Next we had to pull the tarpaulin (patched up with gaffa tape) back over.

I stood on the ridge at one end tugging hand over hand as Janet stayed on the ground and fed the heavy sheet over the eaves.

It took about an hour to get the thing over and as I was looking to get down to tie the corners on this clear and still night (morning), a single, slightly freakish gust of wind caught under the tarp and took the whole thing over the other side of the house.

A wrenching moan escaped Janets lips and we both, once again, felt like crying. She has since said it felt like God playing a trick on us to see just how strong we were.

Back up on the other end ridge, I'm pulling away again and Janet feeding the tarp over the eaves, this time it's harder as it's on the downhill side.

I couldn't see Janet but could hear her gasping, I thought struggling to lift the heavy sheeting.

I eventually got the tarp over the ridge and set about tying it off before any more freakish gusts decided to bless us.

Janet was in a right state, I hadn't realised but her gasping was a genuine panic attack, she had been struggling to breath, the fatigue and tiredness had been too much. She was recovering by the time I found out and made sure she was alright.

Finally securing the tarp, the Moon had disappeared below the horizon, it was 6am, we fell into bed.

The next morning (?) we emerged, bleary eyed at a grey 10.30.

Today we took things easy, well easier. The building was nearly waterproof so we could relax slightly although having got this far, we were seized with a fear that a planning officer would suddenly turn up and bring it all to an abrupt end. Pride had started to creep in, I really wanted to finish the job.

Every strange car winding it's way up the farm track had our attention, willing it not to stop…. and none did.

We fed breathable fabric over the trusses and under the tarp to proof the roof.

After fixing this under the plastic, we decided we could really do with some help for the next job (yes ok, we could really have done with some help with the last few jobs too), which was fixing the corrugated steel roofing sheets.

We found a friend from a neighbouring county who could spend a day with us.

First we put the ceiling beams (4 x 2") up, fixing them across the wall plates, noticing just how uneven the ceiling would eventually be and then the purlins (3 x 2") sitting across the roof trusses.

The next day Dave arrived and was a great help fixing the sheets on the roof.

We had a small dilemma as to whether we should remove the tarp or leave it in place to form an extra water barrier, but then what was the point of the breather membrane? We thought we should have as much vapour permeability as possible but did like the idea of the extra weather proof. A compromise was reached and two strips, roughly 4" wide were cut along just under the ridge, so warm damp air could rise and escape.

It was a fine day towards the end of October and the job almost completed, just the ridge sections to be added the next day.

Inside the floors and walls were drying out. Feeling as if we had battled our way through the storm, we were almost glad we had decided to persevere.

Next came the windows, doors and cladding.

Vertical posts were added running from the floor notches to the wall plate where the windows and door frame were to be fitted.

Of course the bales intruded into the space, not thinking this would be much of a problem, we pulled straw out to enlarge the gap, but of course, this weakened the bales, so on some of them we had to retie or tighten the twines. This is far from easy when the bale is in place. The internal corners I rounded off using a chainsaw, managed to cut through one securing twine. And as I just mentioned this was a bit of a problem. After a lot of messing about, we did manage to get the door and windows in.

Getting the second hand, double glazed windows to work (open, close, you get the idea) was another matter altogether, one window in particular has subsequently occupied several of my days just trying to figure why it's a problem. It's now fixed and working, thank you for asking.

Despite careful planning and picking windows that I thought would fit perfectly, it was perhaps inevitable that the windows, sitting on the first course of bales, weren't the right height to reach the wall plate. They were about 5" too short, so I would have to build a box to fill the gap and stuff it with straw but without the full height kitchen windows, it was threatening to be quite dark inside. Then I thought, let's find out how much it would cost to get two narrow double glazed units built to fit. I found a glazing manufacturer in Hereford and the price was only £15, bargain! Fitted above the existing window they look great and increase the light coming in, even to this day, when I look at these units, I get a little feeling of satisfaction.

The door stuck, it had been out in the rain, swelled and didn't fit in the frame so well. Also it let in water underneath, galvanising my determination to build a porch at some point when we had time. But with furdling and persuading easing and bashing, we got the openings filled and the house secure

and snug.

In less than one month, very nearly just the two of us (with a little help) had built the structure.

We were 'safe', we were water-tight and with the assistance of a portable gas heater borrowed from our local pub, we were slowly drying out.

Chapter 5 – Build, stage 3

We had spent roughly two months in the caravan. It leaked, meaning we couldn't use one end. It was site office, kitchen, bedroom and some where out of the rain. In the mornings the condensation would be running down the walls. Gradually things started to break down. The heater never worked so we had to bring in a gas heater. The hot water broke, meaning we had to heat water on the stove for washing and cooking, it was tiny, grubby (despite constant cleaning) and cluttered. We did have a large awning, which we really needed and kept equipment dry but when the rain came, a small rivulet appeared running through the awning right under the step up to the van. Often this contributed to the general state of damp within boots and the delights of foot rot.

Janet was working weekends as a receptionist down south and so I would drop her off at the terraced house on a Friday and pick her up again on Sunday night, giving us both a chance to bath, do some washing, re-fill water containers, re-charge drill batteries and sort ourselves out.

It also gave us the chance to use a real toilet – oh the luxury!

Back on the field we were using a bucket tucked away in a tent made from 4 stout pieces of hazel forming an aptly named, Tee-Pee. Around this was draped canvas. We had a seat over the bucket, it wasn't that uncomfortable but we did have to crouch under the canvas to get in and out.

After doing your business, you would have to then traipse across to the far side of the big field with a spade.

Daylight was the preferred option, although why a delivery would always turn up at exactly the wrong time I'll never know. However sometimes nature dictated a night-time excursion.

My worst experience was after a long wet day, we were preparing for bed and I decided I couldn't put it off. The wind was blowing, the rain was sheeting down. In full waterproofs off I went to the Tee-pee.

After doing the necessary and re-buttoned up against the weather, I crawled out from under the tent dragging the bucket behind me. It then dawned on me that I needed to pee, so I stopped put the bucket down and undid my waterproofs, it was with a sinking feeling of despair as I watched the wind catch the bucket, sending it rolling across the field, little white sheets of paper flying everywhere. With only a head-torch, I did my best to pick it all up, in the wind and rain, cursing it all, but a small, brown, Richard III was never to be found.

And then there was the night Janet came back exhibiting various stages of terror.

"I was coming back across the big field," she said, "and there were these two green eyes shining back at me in the torch light, watching me, not moving. I moved towards them, expecting the animal – whatever it was, to run away, but it didn't, it just stayed there as if trying to outstare me. I tell you, I ran for it!"

This turned out not to be some fearsome, fearless creature, but most likely a domestic cat.

By this time we had put the plasterboard ceiling up in the smaller of the two rooms and we had been to see Ty Mawr, who are specialists in lime products and sell their own 'straw bale mix' plaster, which is a thick porridge of fat lime putty, water and chopped straw.

For straw bale walls you really need lime plaster for vapour permeability – to let it breath. I had reckoned on needing about one tonne, based on conventional plaster estimates but were told by Ty Mawr, that we would need a minimum of 4 tonne, just for the two base coats,

"Then you also need a top coat."

"Do we?" we asked.

"Well it's not essential but the finish will be quite rough."

"We can live with rough." And in the end the rough finish did work very well, in keeping with the wibbly-wobbly roof, the bendy-wendy ceiling, the wavey cladding and creaking floor. (We're building a Play-School house!)

But hang on, how will the supporting structure cope with all this extra weight, I was worried. Also the price of the stuff was way more than we expected.

In the end we found a compromise, the end walls were well supported by the beams, but the front and back only had two joists to take the weight. So along the front we dug shallow pits between each of the support piers and had to use concrete blocks to create extra piers to support the joists mid span. This just wasn't practical along the back wall, being much higher off the ground, so along the back we dropped battens internally and fixed plasterboard.

The front wall would still be plastered and we bought just two tonne.

I have to say the most impressive thing I found about Ty Mawr was their delivery driver who managed to get his lorry right up onto the field, saving us the effort of hand carrying the wet lime plaster mix, which arrived in jumbo bags ($1m^3$), up from the access track.

We got waney edge Larch cladding from Alun, our friendly local sawmill man, for a very reasonable £500 and it would finish off the exterior perfectly. Apparently Larch, being quite resinous, would not need further weather proofing treatment and so is ideal for our house plus it was very local and low carbon.

Vertical posts were dropped from the wall plate down to the floor plate and to these were fixed the boards, each about ½" thick and 7-9" wide, horizontally overlapping.

Over the next few days we worked it so that when it was wet, we stayed inside putting up the plasterboard, when it was dry, we finished off the cladding outside.

Once the rear wall had been plasterboarded, we brought in a couple of the kitchen units, the worktop with inset sink and a small table top gas stove for cooking, allowing us to use the space as a refuge whilst working on the house and land.

In the caravan life was becoming increasingly uncomfortable. The taps had started to break and the water heater had given up after only three weeks, meaning we had to boil a saucepan for hot water. The awning was in a state of collapse, being propped up with bent poles and gaffa-tape. Plus there simply wasn't the space to do anything. I had whacked my shin slipping on the step after coming in after a late night visit to the toilet Tee-Pee (I still have a scar a year after) but the final straw came one breakfast as I prepared a well earned bowl of cereal after doing a few early morning chores. Balancing it in the narrow space between the sink and the cooker, I moved to get the milk and the slight rock of the van sent my cereal all over the now quite muddy floor. I had had enough, I tried to beat up the caravan but it was surprisingly resilient. After calming down, I decided I would no longer live in this state and on Halloween we moved into our new home. A bed, two fold out chairs and the portable gas heater being our only furniture.

About this time the first of a series of late Autumn gales blew in from the west.

Gusts of 60-70 mph, higher in exposed places. We had chosen our spot well and are shielded from the worst of it by belts of trees to our west, east and north. The south is a little exposed but the field slopes to the north so again giving us some protection.

But our home was built of straw and we all know the story of the three little pigs! We hadn't got around to the soffits or fascia, so there was nothing to stop the wind whipping up and under the tin roof. We laid in bed that night, sleepless, dreading each rising gust as the gale blew through. We could hear the wind hitting the trees and then with a mighty whomph, a gust would hit the house, we could feel the walls shudder and gripped each other tighter. My mind racing away with the possibilities, everything should be secure and strong enough, but what if it wasn't? What if I had made a mistake? We would be in very real danger. Goodness knows what could happen if a wall gave-way or the roof collapse, beside me was the woman I loved who had put her faith in my judgement, if the worst happened it would be my fault. Building Regs are there for a reason.

I desperately wanted it to calm down, wishing the wind to ease, to be able to relax and sleep.

I must have dozed off because around 3am I was woken by the sound of loud flapping outside. I realised the caravan awning, which was still parked beside the house, had completely collapsed, was being caught by the wind and was threatening to turn the caravan over. Janet was also awake, so we both got up and dressed, pulling down the remaining poles, we threw spare, wet bales on the outside to anchor it down until morning and went back to bed.

We survived the night and the storm blew its way past us. It was a massive relief.

The next storm front was due in a couple of days and the forecasts said it may even be worse than the first.

I hurriedly attached extra steel straps or wire rope to the roof trusses and the wall plate.

I fixed fascia planks to the gable ends and even parked the tractor and Landrover across the front to help shield the house from the predicted wind.

Again the storm came overnight, again we laid in bed unable to sleep, feeling each and every gust slamming into the side of the house, wishing it was over.

A number of further storms blew in that winter, one after the other but now we had grown in confidence with our little house's abilities to withstand the forces of nature. But it was a sobering thought that as climate change campaigners, we hadn't given much consideration to the increased energy these storms would carry.

Now we were ready to plaster the interior front and side walls.

Lime plaster doesn't dry like conventional plaster, it carbonates over time meaning it absorbs carbon dioxide and becomes harder but it must not be applied below 5-7 degs C for this to work properly.

Although winter was approaching, it was still mild and us living in the house meant keeping some heating going. As temps dropped at night, we huddled around a Super Ser gas heater on one bar watching the thermometer and dreaming of insulating the loft, but that's the next story.

So the book says that lime plaster sticks really well to straw, you can rub it in with your hands but do not add water to the lime plaster mix or else it may crack. My cousin – a plasterer – said the first coat needs to be very runny and you flick the slurry at the walls.

The mix we got was not runny so should we add water?

We phoned Ty Mawr and they said slap it hard into the straw.

We should have listened to my cousin.

It was a nightmare.

I had previously gone over the walls with a hedge trimmer attachment on a strimmer to give it a hair cut, cutting off the longer sticky-out bits of straw. But as we slapped the plaster on, it just bounced off again.

We hired a cement mixer and ran the plaster through that for 15 mins. It still would not stay on the walls and I started to wonder at the advice we had been given. I phoned my cousin,

"Run it through the mixer for at least half an hour or it will never stick," he said, so the next day we did and it certainly helped.

But the plastering was still an awful job. We could only get it on handful by handful (wearing gloves of course because the stuff is really quite caustic, indeed I had a little bare skin exposed above my wrist which came out in a nasty sore), and rubbing it in, every third handful falling off. I used a plastic trowel which was a bit quicker, some advice we read was not to use a plastic one but, as it turned out, it was fine.

After about 5 days we had completed our first coat and it was starting to harden, so we moved onto the second coat. This went on much easier, having a decent base to cling to but time was spent trying to smooth over the surface. Of course the final effect would be lumpy-bumpy as it followed the contours of the bales and ratchet straps that we've left in place and trowel marks are still plainly visible but visitors seem to love the rough earthy feel, as we do too.

If we had to do the plastering all over again (please no), I would take roughly a quarter of a tonne of the stuff, mix in water to make a runny slurry and flick onto the walls as my cousin recommended, allow a week or so for that to firm up, then slap in 1 tonne of Ty Mawr's straw bale mix after running through the cement mixer for at least half an hour, at a thickness of about 10-15mm to give a base coat, then once the base had hardened sufficiently, the remaining ¾ tonne be applied to a less thick depth.

Once the plaster had hardened, and with the cladding finished, the walls gained rigidity and the storm fronts no longer sent shock waves through the building.

Chapter 6 – Making a Comfy Home

In between the drudgery of sticking handfuls of lime plaster on the walls, picking it off the floor and re-slamming it into the straw with ever increasing frustration, we were trying to organise the loft insulation.

Loft Insulation.

A friend of ours, Anthony, had promised us a large quantity of proper sheep's wool insulation (also originating from Ty Mawr) which he had left over from a project. But we couldn't seem to get hold of him.

We suspected it wouldn't be enough to cover our 70 sq.m loft to the depth of 250 – 300mm which we were after, so we ordered up a pallet of Warmcell 100 which is shredded up newspaper, treated with a fire retardant. Insulation is really expensive, especially if you're trying to make it as environmentally friendly as possible.

Initially this stuff was a joy to work with, open the packet into which it had been compressed and fluff the stuff out with your hands, spreading it all around. I found the best technique was to dig it out of the bags as a dog or burrowing rabbit would.

Quite dusty, we would emerge from the roof space covered in a fine layer of paper and smelling of W.H.Smiths.

But it does have a significant down-side. Late one evening I was up in the loft, spreading the insulation and I lost my balance on a ceiling beam, putting my hand down to steady myself onto plasterboard, the whole 8 x 4' sheet fell, taking with it about 2 cubic meters of loose, fluffy Warmcell, all over our bed below. I now know that the stuff is really difficult to clean up and spent the night sneezing.

We had some EarthWool left over from the floor insulation so we laid that around the outer edges to confine the Warmcell and stop it blowing away with the draught from up under the eaves. Although some re-organisation was required after the gales had blown through.

We still couldn't get hold of Anthony and we were starting to feel the cold in there. We were getting desperate, should we bite the bullet and spend out on a whole heap more insulation?

Then the news broke that 30 Greenpeace activists had been arrested by Russian Federal Security Service in International waters up in the Arctic.

They were protesting against the Russian oil company, Gazprom, who were preparing to drill for oil.

Anthony was one of those detained. He was taken to a prison in Murmansk and was awaiting a hearing, charged with piracy. I phoned his partner, she was understandably upset and very worried, we all were and we prayed that he would be soon on his way home.

The hearings didn't go well, they all would be held for another 3 months to allow for their cases to be fully investigated (and Gazprom to complete their drilling), they were further charged with hooliganism. This didn't bode well, in 2012 three women of the punk group Pussy Riot were sentenced to 2 years each in prison for hooliganism – performing a protest song in a Moscow cathedral, and Russia seemed to be becoming increasingly interested in extending it's frontiers, especially with regards to Arctic resources. Russian prisons are tough places, stories emerge of poor food, forced labour and endemic TB.

As the weeks slipped by, I regularly called Anthony's partner and eventually broached the subject of the insulation, she said she would try to get a message to him.

The reply came back from Ant with surprise that we had built the house already and that yes we should help ourselves to the insulation stored in his barn, in return he wanted 2 weeks help the following year building his woodland workshop. Fair exchange I thought, still hoping that he would be at liberty next year.

I'm thinking there must be very few houses in the country whose insulation had to be ordered from a Russian prison cell via diplomatic channels!

A little later, just after Christmas, we heard that the Arctic 30, as they had become known, would be released, first on bail, then all charges dropped in a sweeping amnesty ahead of the up-coming Winter Olympics Russia would be hosting. It appeared they weren't keen to have human rights issues marring their moment and Anthony was home by the New Year.

Anyway, we went and got the insulation and fitted it on top of the Warmcell. The single bar gas heater was keeping the temperature inside the house above 8 degs, occasionally reaching the sweltering heights of 12 degs at which times we would strip off our winter coats and put our feet up in front of the heater, wet socks drying above and inquisitively poke the damp plaster. Luxury, (compared to the caravan).

With the internal walls up, a little gas stove to cook on and washing water being pumped in, I now set about building a proper, indoor compost toilet.

Compost Toilet.
We had looked at lots of designs, read about how compost loo's work and noted that we needed to separate out the urine from the faeces. There are simple, and expensive devices for doing this but we didn't like the way they worked. So we went even simpler, two toilets – one for solids, one for liquids.

Solids (including paper) would go into a plastic dustbin sited in the space under the house. The liquids would go down a pipe to a soakaway in the ground at the back of the house.

We found the size bins we needed and ordered 3 off the internet.

We waited with anticipation of having an indoor loo.

We waited with growing frustration, but the delivery window was over two weeks, the two weeks of Christmas, bank holidays and all.

New Year came but the bins didn't, so I contacted the supplier,

"Yep, they were delivered about a week ago."

"Well we haven't got them so where are they?"

"I'll check with the driver."

Some hours later he called back,

"Driver said he left them at your mobile home, just inside the picket fence."

"Err, that's not us, but I think I know who it is. I'll go and see if I can find them."

A neighbour up the track was living in such a home but why had he not brought them down to us as surely the bins would have been labelled with our names? He was Turkish and giving him the benefit of doubt as to how well he could read English, we went to see him.

"Oh yes, I've put my dog biscuits in them! I thought the Council left them and so I thought great, somewhere to put my dog biscuits."

"But they're ours, can you please give them to us?"

"Yes, yes," he said in a slightly unconvincing manner. "I'll drop them down to you tomorrow, but first I have to get some sacks to put the dog biscuits in, they're big dogs you know."

"Okay, tomorrow."

Looking forward to being able to defecate in peace, in our own bathroom, we waited, wondering about this man up the lane.

I had built a platform for the seats in the bathroom and cut two holes in the floor. We had come across a piece of serious drainpipe, 300mm wide, twin wall plastic, this would be the poop shute. I fixed the seat to an OSB board covered with Foamex plastic with the hole cut in, to that I fixed the drainpipe/shute. The other end would be fixed to the lid of the dustbin, also with the hole cut out, obviously. The lid sat on the bin. To change bins would be a simple matter of unclipping the lid and lifting the seat/board/shute/lid assembly, whip the bin out and new one back under.

The next day came and went, as did the following. We went to see the man up the lane, now prepared to get arsey.

"Oh yes, I'm sorry, I've so much work on at the moment, fitting security lights, I'll drop them down tomorrow."

"Tomorrow, promise?"

"Yes promise, of course, first thing."

Grrrrr.

But the next day, bright and earlier, he was good to his word and appeared with the bins. Well, we had got them at last and the construction of our poo loo was complete.

To the bin lid I attached another pipe (68mm guttering down-pipe) to allow gas, smells and vapour to escape. Into this pipe I've now fitted a small fan (a 12v computer processor cooling fan) which is connected to the batteries via the solar controller.

Nine months later and we have two full bins happily composting and the third under the house, is nearly full so we've bought an extra one because the first isn't ready to be emptied around the fruit trees just yet.

(as a post script to this, we're finding there's still too much moisture in the bins and we'll have to adapt them somehow to solve this, probably by fitting a false bottom so that any liquid can separate and settle/evaporate)

I still wasn't sure how to channel the pee yet and as my mind wandered over various ways of how to get a wide hole – under the toilet seat – down to a small pipe, we happened to be driving to town when we passed a discarded traffic cone. The base had probably been run over and was missing but it left a funnel, perfect for our purpose.

The inverted traffic cone was now screwed to the underside of the board, next to the poo shute. Seat fitted over and an offset bend into a 68mm guttering pipe fitted to the top (now bottom) of the cone. This then took the liquid to a pit part filled with stones and covered with earth.

We had indoor facilities – what pleasure! (Being a bloke from the sticks, I still prefer to pee outside but not necessarily in the middle of the night!)

Internal doors, either bought cheap from the local auction or from my sisters house renovation, were installed along with kitchen units, an Ebay bath and wash basin.

When my sister, decided to replace the kitchen in the house she had just bought, I grabbed the opportunity to save the old units for our new build.

Over a year later, after having been pulled apart, stored in a barn and then under a sweating plastic tarpaulin, a lot of the chipboard was bowed, rotting or broken. We managed to salvage a couple of units, the worktop and sink.

Kitchen and bath taps also survived.

Water.

So next came the plumbing.

This seemed to take forever. I'm no plumber, don't enjoy it, things tend to leak in my experience, but I do know the basics.

Three water tanks were arranged around the back and side of the building. Two, 1,000 litre tanks came from Ebay – old orange juice containers apparently – which would store washing water and one 2,500 litre tank bought new as it was purposely made for above ground potable (drinkable) water.

Guttering was fixed to the roof truss ends, weaving in and out as it followed the contours of the bale walls and ending in down-pipes leading into the water tanks.

Little pieces of plastic mesh were put over the holes into the tanks to try to reduce the amount of debris going in.

For the drinking water I really wanted to minimise the opening to the tank and the amount of crap going in so I needed a seal-able food safe plastic box in which to feed the rain water that could then have a pipe half way up the side to supply the tank, thus allowing heavier items to sink to the bottom of the box and regularly cleaned. My first thought was Tupperware but it needed to be opaque to stop algae growing.

Then we discovered and expensive brand of ice cream that came in a black box that would be ideal. I know plastic isn't the best stuff to store water in, I'm sure some plastics are better than others, for example you are not meant to reuse the bottles posh spring water comes in, but we all do. The potable water tank was plastic and I considered that the water within the ice cream box would only be there for a short time, although as I write this, I realise we haven't had rain for about a week and so that same small quantity of water would be sitting in the tub doing what I don't know. Maybe I should re-think this detail.

We have actually chosen a preference for plastic plumbing over copper for our drinking system as we suspect it's less harmful.

Drinking water is drawn out of the bottom of the tank by a pressure regulated diaphragm pump (when you open a tap, the pressure drops and the pump operates). It then goes through a string filter, ceramic filter and then a carbon filter. The ceramic one should stop 99% of bacteria but we found it was clogging too quickly with bits of dirt meaning we had to change it every couple of months and so we added the string filter to try to stop the dirt reaching the ceramic. At the time of writing, it seems to be working and we've had the same filter in for about 3 months now. We have a special little tap for drinking water.

The washing water is pumped up to a loft header tank from the two exterior (orange juice) tanks. The pump being controlled by a float switch (designed for boat bilge pumps) which operates when the water level in the header tank drops. Water then falls by gravity to the bath, basin and kitchen cold taps, it also fills the hot water tank, but we'll come to that a little later.

To my amazement, this all seemed to work, and no serious leaks.

Now a word about power –

Electricity.

I do have some expertise in this field, I've trained in engineering and worked as a maintenance fitter and production technician but I do not have the necessary tickets to do 240v installations.

I wanted a 12v system for the house, it's not the most efficient but there are lots of devices and equipment readily available and it's safer, and we wouldn't have to drag in an electrician to sign it all off.

For now I took a cable from the caravan which was being powered by solar panels and leisure batteries and set up a makeshift distribution panel using a block of automotive spade fuses, inside the front door.

I had put off the installation of the lights as being of lower importance than other jobs (we'd got used to wearing headtorches as our de rigueur accessories) but when I got around to it, the thrill of switching on the lights that evening came as a little surprise. Suddenly the house changed from being a shell to a home.

Whilst building the house, we occasionally needed more power than the cordless drill could provide, The generator had become really hard to start and then it's starting cord snapped. We bought a cheap, modified sine wave, 2000w inverter off the internet.

Within a week it broke. We were sent a replacement. That lasted less than a week. All we were using was an electric drill! Lesson learned; not to use equipment knocked out cheap from China (have since found that this is virtually impossible now-a-days).

We now run any 240v appliances from a rather expensive 1200w, pure sine wave inverter, and make sure they do not exceed 1000w.

This includes the fridge, laptop, cordless chargers, a small travel iron, angle grinder, CD player and hair clippers.

The water pumps, loo fan and lights are all 12v.

I'm still amazed at how little energy the LED bulbs we've fitted use, they hardly make any difference to the batteries' charge.

We've since fitted four solar panels on the roof of the porch and replaced the leisure batteries (which literally fell apart) with four newer ones from the same source. This is currently managing to supply all out needs except we have to keep turning the fridge on and off. Come winter I feel the lack of solar power will impact our fridge most of all and so we are looking at adapting a chest freezer by running it at above the freezing point. I've heard this will save loads of energy and the air inside will stay cooler.

If we need more power, all we have to do is upgrade the system, more solar panels, up-rate the controller, perhaps a small wind turbine for the winter months and more batteries.

Grey Water Waste.

A year previously, we had commissioned a design for a reed bed system for disposing of the grey water – waste water from washing – from a consultant at the Centre for Alternative Technology in Machynlleth, West Wales. It consisted of a filter tank, two vertical reed beds to total 4 cubic meters (quite small as we weren't discharging that much water with the few appliances we were going to have) and a tertiary treatment through a horizontal bed.

This design we presented to Natural Resources Wales, our version of the Environment Agency. After some delay and a few phone calls, it transpired that there was confusion over which office should be dealing with us, we were getting directed to the English office who batted us back to the Welsh one. It appeared that the NRW, being relatively new, were still in the throws of getting themselves organised.

Eventually they decided that we needed a permit. So I applied, paid the fee and waited.

They contacted me to say that they thought we didn't need the horizontal bed as it would be discharging into a wetland area (a boggy bit of woodland that collects the water from the field), so long as it was going through a settlement tank before the reed beds, it would be fine and I got the permit.

Ahead of the house build, I installed three insulated, ex frozen fish transport tanks. Each about 2 cubic meters. One would become the settlement and filter tank, the other two reed beds.

Carefully we built up the layers of pipes, stones, gravel and sand as instructed.

Now as I looked at the waste pipe exiting the house, I realised that it was slightly lower than the first tank. There was no way around it, the pipes had to have a downhill run and the tanks weighing well over a tonne each were firmly rooted to the ground. I could empty the tanks and relocate them or lower the first tank and add a pump in between it and the beds, which is what I went for.

The pump was a 'gulper' boat bilge pump that should cope with the sort of gunk that floats off down domestic waste water pipes. Added to that was another float switch to control the pump. It worked, for about a week. Also I didn't like these big ugly tanks sitting beside the house. So one weekend, while Janet was away working, I decided to move them.

I started emptying them, soon hitting gravel and stones. The spade just wasn't working and it seemed that I would have to take the stones out in handfuls! It was going to be an almost impossible, time consuming task. But these tanks look pretty strong, where I want them is downhill, I wonder if I could move them still full?

I dug out my Dads old turfer winch that he used to use for felling awkward trees, wrapped a strong rope, many times, around a tree in the general direction I wanted the tanks to go and started winching. Bit by bit, inch by inch they moved, grinding their way through the soft soil. Moving to a new tree I could change the direction and angle until both tanks were in place. It had taken all day but it was with sense of achievement that I nonchalantly mentioned to Janet on her return,

"Oh yeah, I moved the reed beds, think they look better there."

Finding the correct reeds to plant in the beds was the next challenge. Garden centres are few and far between around here, none of them stocked the reeds (unsurprisingly I suppose), so I ordered twenty off the internet, wondering how the would survive the postal system. They arrived, looking a bit worse for wear and we planted them. They died, or so we thought, a few have re-sprouted and we're hoping they will continue to colonise the beds. I should probably plant some more though.

Heat.

The heart of the house, the wood burning stove. We wanted something that we could use to cook, provide hot water and keep us warm in the winter, but it couldn't be so stupidly heavy so that it would punch it's way through the floor and we had to be able to manhandle into position. After some internet research, we realised we could afford a brand new but basic make of stove called Prity, from Bulgaria. Apparently they are very popular in Germany and the majority of customer reviews were good. Made of steel rather than the cast iron of traditional ranges, they weighed in at around 130kgs and are far cheaper an Aga or Rayburn. There was even a retailer not too far from us (only about 2 hours drive, not far for Wales). So we decided to go and have a look.

I tried to call them to see which models they stocked, no answer. It was the weekend so I left it until Monday morning. I phoned again, no answer. The plaster was on the walls, we were sleeping in the bedroom, it was starting to get distinctly chilly and the gas heater was going through bottles. I was dreaming of having a wood burning stove, hot water, comfort and wanted to just go out and get one. Of course I realised we wouldn't be able to fire the thing up until we had the back boiler all plumbed in and working, but I wanted to crack on with it anyway.

So I checked the retailers website – only open 11am-5pm, Wednesday to Sunday (no explanation apparent why they weren't answering the phone over the weekend).

Wednesday morning, at 10am, we jumped in the car and set off. I phoned again at 11.10, 11.30, 11.40 no answer. We were virtually there when someone did pick up, yes they had Pritys but the model names were confusing, at least it wouldn't be a wasted trip.

We arrived, they had two models, not the one I had wanted, these were higher kw outputs but I wasn't going to leave without one. We settled on the model with two glass doors, one for the fire, one for the oven which sits directly over the fire. We have found that this arrangement gives better heat to the oven but not much good for heating saucepans on the top. Still this works for us as we can use a small gas hob for that.

We did a deal for cash and to take the stove away there and then. We had to borrow a couple of blokes from the boatyard and loaded it into the back of our (estate) car.

Arriving home we realised getting it in the house would be a challenge. By now the house was surrounded by deep mud. Just walking around the place had become annoying and tiresome.

We had a number of pallets lying around which the straw bales had sat on, so we lined them up from the back of the car to the front door. Working the 130kg stove out of the rear of the car, we tilted it upright onto the first pallet, then 'walked' it over the pallets to the front door. Using an extra pallet got it up to the level of the interior and we were in. We had put a slab of marble (something we had found in our old house which looked like it had once graced a butchers counter or wall even), in the chosen position and we 'walked' the stove to sit upon it, now realising that to get the pipes in and out of the back of it would be a right pfaff but that would be for another day.

The next job was to get the back boiler and hot water tank plumbed in. We got in touch with a HETAS registered plumber who came out, sucked his teeth a bit, then said he was really busy at the moment, I tentatively suggested that I could do most of the work and he could check it all over to finish it off. I had thought of mimicking my Dads system which is quite simple, gravity fed, thermo-syphoning, direct flow. But the plumber said no, we had to have an indirect system which meant more work.

I am aware I've suddenly dropped in a host of technical terms which, if you really want to understand it, I'll have to explain as best I can.

Usually water flows under pressure into a header tank (plastic tank in the loft), that acts as a reservoir in case the water pressure fails. We are pumping the rain water from the water tanks (at ground level), up to the header tank. In a direct flow system, the water comes out of the tank, by gravity, into the back boiler on the stove, heats up, then rises (hot water rises) up pipes to the hot water cylinder (thermo-syphoning), filling the cylinder with lovely hot water.

An indirect system has a second header tank which fills the back boiler, heats up, rises, then goes through a coil of pipe within the hot water cylinder, transferring it's heat to the colder water around the coil. It then circulates back to the boiler via a radiator to dissipate excess heat – stop the system boiling. This water stays continuously within this set of pipes and has anti-corrosion chemicals added to it.

We had to follow the plumbers advice and so I set to work.

The stove had a higher kw rating than I had anticipated, so the radiator had to be quite large to accommodate the potential heat the thing could throw out. As we were sourcing most of our stuff second-hand, we ended up with three radiators, one for each room (bathroom, bedroom and living room) although we seldom need to turn on the living room one as the stove is in the kitchen area within the living room and when we do the plastic pipes go all bendy.

Full days were spent trying to work out all the bits I needed and ordering them online. Then more days were spent cutting, joining and fitting pipes, tanks, cylinder, valves and taps. Days turned into weeks. Finally the day came to fill and test the system.

Only two leaking joints, I was well impressed.

The flue pipe was single wall steel for the first meter then twin wall (insulated) from there on up through the roof. A proper flashing plate and a home made cowl (an inverted stainless steel dog bowl) is meant to keep the rain out but when it comes down heavy with wind, rain still manages to make it's way down to the stove despite half a tube of mastic. (I've since figured out it needed a storm collar).

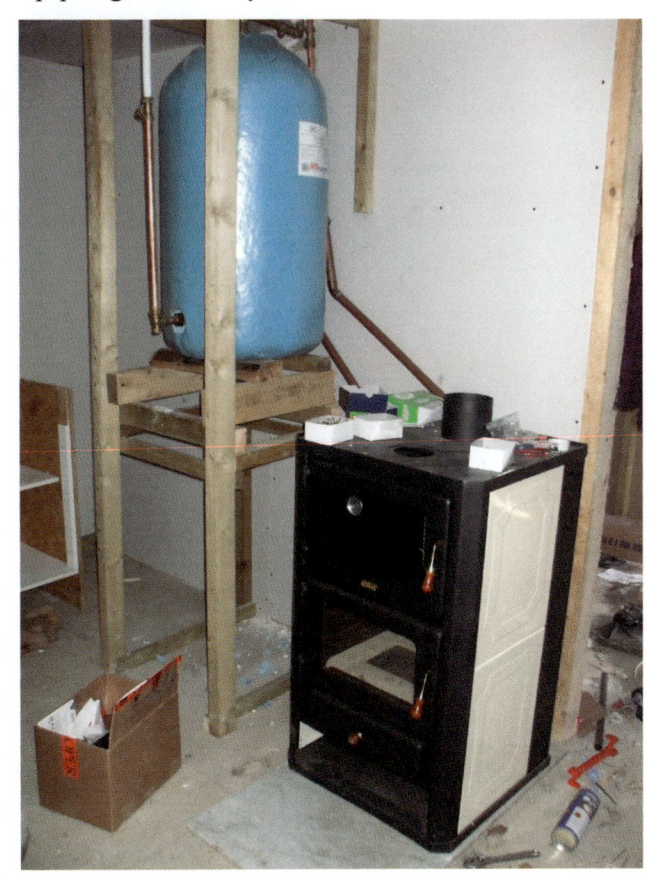

I fixed the leaky joints and with some trepidation, we lit the fire.

The water in the secondary system – that's the one that goes through the back boiler – was heating but it wasn't thermo-syphoning, it wasn't circulating, it was just getting hotter and hotter. There must be an airlock in the system so we let the fire die down and I opened various valves and 'cracked' joints to let the air out until water flowed. I was confident now that water filled every bit of the pipework.

The next day we lit the fire again, this time the radiator in the bathroom warmed nicely but still no heat transfer to the water cylinder. Perhaps we just weren't getting it hot enough, so we put more logs on. Now it got really hot, the temperature on the oven thermometer read 200, the water in the secondary system started making noises, it rattled, it bubbled, then thumped. We ran outside fearing something untoward might happen. A whooshing sound came from the loft and the noises stopped. Gently closing down the fire, we investigated and found that the expansion pipe had done it's job, scolding hot water had gone up and out, splattering back to the small header tank. The expansion pipe runs from the top of the secondary system and it's open end rises above the header. It ensures that if the water boils, the expanded water has somewhere to go.

So now I completely undid the pipes going into and out of the hot water cylinder. Water came out of the one going in, so I reconnected it, but no water was coming out of the other. It just didn't make sense, how can water not go downhill?

The only thing that could stop it, I figured, was an airlock within the coil.

This time I drained the system, actually removing all the pipes to the hot water cylinder, then slowly refilling until water started to flow, then reconnecting each pipe in turn. Finally water reached the top joint and I resealed it. Now surely no air was present.

We lit the fire and sat back with the radiator valve fully open for safety sake. Nope, still no hot water. Arrgghh.

Once again I worked through all the joints, was that an escape of air on that last one, the tortuously difficult to get at joint on the top of the cylinder? Perhaps…. Yes, warm water was starting to flow back down the return pipe, now it would only be a matter of time and the luxury of piped hot water.

The subsequent bath was divine.

Porch.

We needed a porch. I didn't realise until we started using the house, how much we needed one. The very nice (second-hand) front door had swollen and was sticking but still allowing rain in under. Our muddy boots had to be left on a muddy square of breather membrane just inside, the chipboard floor was becoming saturated.

The winter was turning into one long slog of rain. It never seemed to stop, one of the wettest on record. The plus side of this was that it stayed mild, only one morning did we see a light dusting of snow and even frosts were few and far between. The downside was mud, lots of it, everywhere.

Anthony had been released from Russia and was keen to see our progress. He turned up bearing gifts of 6 x 4' plywood covered pallets for us to use as duckboards over the mud. But what I saw was our new porch.

I picked out the best five and carefully separated the chipboard tops. Two would become the floor and three the roof.

The front corners are 7' fence posts from the local agricultural merchants, sunk 2' into the ground, giving a slope almost matching the roof.

The porch roof was covered with shed felt then the solar panels, wired to the controller and four deep cycle batteries in a plastic garden storage box.

One side is open onto a small kind of veranda, the other two with windows (remember the full length double glazed units that we couldn't use because the wall kept falling down?) and waney edge cladding. Have porch, now happy.

Still got lots of mud though.

Chapter 7 – Wrapping Up

Spring eventually came, the walls lime-washed and we started to enjoy our new home.

We were looking out for second hand laminate flooring but nothing of the quantity we wanted (65 sq.m) was forthcoming. Because we lost the extra window in kitchen area, we needed to use all the light now entering the remaining windows and keep the décor white or very pale. Looking around B&Q, a white wood effect laminate caught Janet's eye but was really expensive.

A couple of weeks later, 100 sq.m of the same stuff came up on Ebay, had been used for only 3 weeks in an exhibition hall. We had to go to Swindon to get it but it was perfect.

Decorating progressed through to summer.

And now, having battled through the hard times, the frustrations, the despair, the mud, the all-nighters, the mental breakdown, the physical pain and the grumps, we're very happy in our off-grid home.

We are still sometimes woken in the middle of the night by field mice getting into the straw and roof space, I'm sorry to say that we have resorted to traps.

A number of things are being improved as we go along and there are more things to maintain or manage than your usual energy hungry house but that's fine so long as you're happy to change the poo bin when it's full and know what to do if the tone of the water pumps tells you that one of the tanks is empty.

Despite the problems we encountered, there is a real pleasure to looking around and seeing each bit that you created. A sense of achievement of course but also a little tingle remains when coming in at dusk to a reassuring warmth and switching on the lights.

Fini?

Post Script

Five years have now passed and the house is still standing!

Indeed, the structure remains exactly as it was when first built - slightly bendy but strong.

An embodied energy analysis has shown that, by using recycled and natural materials wherever possible, the construction was carbon neutral. The biggest culprit was the tin roof which was offset by locking up carbon within the straw and timber.

The financial cost was in the region of £12,000

All power for electricity and lighting is from solar photovoltaic panels. Heat and hot water comes from a solar thermal panel or our wood stove, making it zero carbon in use.

And no, we still haven't heard from the planning office.

Printed by Amazon Italia Logistica S.r.l.
Torrazza Piemonte (TO), Italy